Going Around with Bachelors

Going Around
with Bachelors

Agnes Walsh

For Cherie,
a small bit
of Newfoundland.
Enjoy. Agnes

Brick Books

National Library of Canada Cataloguing in Publication

Walsh, Agnes, 1950–
    Going around with bachelors / Agnes Walsh.

Poems.
Accompanied by a CD.

ISBN-13: 978-1-894078-56-6
ISBN-10: 1-894078-56-X

I. Title.

PS8595.A5846G63 2007   C811'.54   C2006-906536-5

We acknowledge the Canada Council for the Arts, the Government of Canada through the Book Publishing Industry Development Program (BPIDP), and the Ontario Arts Council for their support of our publishing program.

Cover image © Martin Cormier. Vue 2, from the series 36 Vues du Mont Sainte-Ann. Digital painting, ink jet printing on paper, 90 x 120 cm., 2005.

Author photograph by Ned Pratt.

The book is set in Minion and Helvetica.

Design and layout by Alan Siu.

Printed and bound by Sunville Printco Inc.

Brick Books
431 Boler Road, Box 20081
London, Ontario N6K 4G6

www.brickbooks.ca

For Patrick and Simone

CONTENTS

I Solemn

My mother scrubbed my face and braided my hair.
She told me to put on my dark blue corduroy dress,
the good thick one from Aunt Mary. She laid the crescent
of hat on her head and stuck a long white pin
with a pearled end into it. (And her head?) It
went in so deep but she didn't jump or cry out, or even wince.
What she did was pull the veil down from its fold until
it rested against her nose.

And gloves. Hers black and mine white.
"You must be very serious. And don't be scared, there's
nothing to be scared about. It's only death, and death can't
hurt you." She took me by the hand and closed the door
behind us and turned the key.

It was my first time for death. I was thought big enough.
So we walked down Swan's road to Mrs. Corrigan's.
The sun was all hallelujah and gave the grass that warm,
green smell. My friends were swinging in the playground,
singing "itsy bitsy teenee weenee yellow polka-dot bikini
that she wore for the first time today." "Look straight ahead,"
my mother said, "be solemn." And I was, although my shoes
pinched. I looked at the clouds moving
fast in the sky above and felt that shiver of life
when it holds you and shakes you between not knowing
and knowing *something*.

Men were outside the door smoking cigarettes
with tams pushed back, dressed up like Sunday.
One man moved himself off the door frame and said "Alice."

Mom said "Francis." Inside was like going into dark night.
The room was full of women and two nuns. Along the back
wall a long, black, shiny box, sleek as a trout. There were
rosary beads on laps and faces flattened with sorrow.

Up! I was swooped up and held above the box and
inside was the meringue of a lemon pie and a woman
lying in the meringue. Not really Mrs. Corrigan who used to
yell and chase us with the broom and tell us we should be
tied to the clothesline. She was far away, tired and cold.
"Kiss her on the hands," my mother whispered. My lips
felt pink, her hands felt white.

On the floor again I was given a triangle of ham sandwich
and a saucer of hot, sweet tea. "She's a grand good girl now
after going to a poor soul's wake." And all the women smiled
sorrowfully at me. And I solemn.

Solemn as could be.

The Laying Out, 1956

Wash the corpse, put on the habit,
put the pennies on the eyelids,
the prayer book under the jaw,
fold the arms with the rosary beads
entwined around the fingers,
stop the clock, turn the looking glass
to the wall, knock him on the forehead
with the hammer to make sure he's dead.

Almost a Word

I was twenty-four years old and not married and that was old for those times. I was working for a man as his housekeeper and I worked hard six and a half days a week. He gave me a couple of hours off on Sunday to go to Mass. It was a steady go to keep up with the work. I hauled water five times a day, and used an old flat iron heated up on the back of the stove. One Sunday after Mass the old man told me to keep on my good dress and to wait a spell in the kitchen. So I sat down on the daybed with my hands folded in my lap and waited. Before long a man came in and he took a chair by the door and him and the old man started talking about weather, fish, and old schooners up the bay. The young fellow never looked at me and he never spoke a word to me. Then he got up and they shook hands and said good-bye. The old man said the young fellow's name was Bill and that he worked on the Labrador. He said he came home in the fall of the year to take care of his old aunt who was going to leave him the house when she died. He told me that this Bill was dependable, never drank, and always paid up his accounts. I said to myself, well, that's all very well and good, but what's that got to do with me?

Well, the exact same thing went on the next Sunday, and the Sunday after that. On the third Sunday, I tell you, I was in no mood to go sitting around like a bump on a log listening to the two of them. So, I don't know, I must have tapped my foot, or cleared my throat real loud or something, because Bill looked over at me and said, "Would you like to be going for a walk up the road with me?" Well, in those days you never went walking with a boy alone unless you were hooked up with him. Oh, it might be all right to run into a few fellows if you were with a pack of girls. You might call out to one another. But I knew something was up when he asked me that.

So anyway, we walked up around the church. He never said a word. When I said, "Lovely weather" he kicked at a rock, gentle-like gave it a kick. He was never rough. That kick seemed to be almost a word, almost a conversation. We were coming back down around when Harry O'Keefe came out from behind a shed and started walking alongside me. Bill moved in around the back of us and wedged in between myself and Harry. "Move over, Harry," he said, "she's my woman." Harry went on then and Bill walked me home. When we got to the gate he took a ring out of his pocket and he put it on my finger. "There you go, love," he said, "we're engaged now. We'll get married in the fall when I get back off the Labrador." Then he put his hand in his pocket again and drew out an envelope and handed it to me. "There's a bit of money in there. Buy yourself a nice suit and a hat to get married in."

So that's what I did. We got married the next fall and we stayed married for fifty years. He was never much of a man for talking but that suited me just fine.

Dad and the Fridge Box

My father never wanted anything. Everything was a fight, Mom said. He didn't want the telephone and he still doesn't know how to talk on it. He didn't want the television but now where is he every Friday night but plunked down in the parlor watching Cher. He wouldn't miss it for Mass. He definitely didn't want the refrigerator. He thought it was only a gadget to fill up space.

Mom was fidgety the day it was due to arrive from town. She kept going to the door to look out and she kept drying her hands on her apron when they weren't even wet. "Where's your father now?" she kept asking over her shoulder. "In the shed," I kept saying. Finally it came and was landed on our doorstep. The men never brought it in so Mom had to go out and get Dad to help us put it on one of the old throw mats and haul and push it into the kitchen. He was looking at it with a funny glint in his eye. Not a mad look, but something else and I couldn't tell what it was. When we had it shoved in the corner, back up against the wall, he kept saying, "Careful now. Mind, mind." I thought to myself, Jeez, he's glad we got it. Imagine that! Mom started cutting at the cardboard box with the bread knife when Dad said "No, no, let me at it." He was so careful, took so long I thought Mom would blow a gasket. He only cut the front of the box away, would not cut the sides or the top or the bottom. "For God's sake, Bill," Mom said. "I know what I'm at," he said to her. It was hard to get the fridge out because there was hardly any place to put our hands in order to grab ahold to it. Finally we had to haul and wedge it out by the open door of it.

When we had it out Dad backed down the hall with the box in tow. He never even looked at the fridge. He took his chair out of its spot in the parlour and put the fridge box in its place. Then he got one of Mom's braided mats and put it on the floor of the box and then he put his chair in the box. And that's where he sat every time he sat in the parlor. Mom said, "Bill, you're not going sitting in that box?" "It's cozy," Dad said, "it keeps the drafts off me." You see, my father was a man obsessed with keeping warm. He even used to put his tools in the oven at night so they'd be warm for the morning. We'd say, "Dad, your hammer is ready. Dad, your saw is done." Men would come to visit him as he sat in his box. They'd say, "That's a dandy box you got there Bill b'y." No one paid much mind to it. No one thought it was odd. Because, you see, that was a time when the old people used everything.

Going Around with Bachelors

That night your sister came round
to my back door with the November wind
lashing her long black hair around her face,
and her talking through her hair to me,

was the first time I met her
and she was telling me to come to you,
because you were pouring everything liquid down the drain,
you had your mother a prisoner of fright in her own home,

and I went following your sister out into the pitch black
because the storm knocked all the lights down. Her saying you
had an aeroplane ticket to Sweden, the land of free love.
What does that mean? she asked, leaning into my arm,
me traipsing after her up the ladder to the kitchen window
because you'd barred all the doors. You standing at the sink

looking over your shoulder at me. Your mother with the rosary beads
pulled tight across her knuckles and hoping
I'd be the ticket to you stopping all you were doing. You saying,
"Since you left me I'm a free man now." And me saying "Peter,
you're free, yes, and all of us your captives. Hand me over the tin
of milk and hand me over your passport." And Jesus, I swore then,
I'll never go around with another bachelor.

To Boston

We were going down to O'Keefe's,
myself and Paddy Cochrane, when
he got turned from the idea
and took the path back up the hill.

I went ahead on my own, I figured
to go in for a spell and have a look,
and when I got there I saw
the dancers having a break
and you fanning yourself with
your head thrown back, laughing
at Micky Houlihan's profound fucking wit.

Outside I inhaled the night's sharp smack,
hugged the coat around me,
had a smoke at Kitty's Pinch
where the sound of the water trickling
was no comfort, and I thought, as I flicked
the butt into the bog, Ah Christ, tomorrow
it's the boat for Boston and leave her to Mick,
and have her wondering—"Whatever happened
to Ag Welsh?"

Homecoming to the End

That way he had of looking over his glasses at me
when I tried to say something matter-of-fact,
but knew I wasn't pulling it off.
He wouldn't say anything, would never answer right away,
just go back to his paper
and say it to the print, matter-of-fact.

I told him I was going to marry a sailor
and go away. He said: "Go away?
To where you know no one?"
That stopped me, made me lonely
before I'd made the steady plans.
"It's your life, and you can always change
your mind," he said.
He made it difficult to rebel.

Years later, he rowed us across Southeast Arm.
With the sail up, the air felt softer on the skin,
the mind relaxed into a carefree sinking.
The open canvas flapped in the wind,
billowing out like a blossoming magnolia.
As he coasted us in, I trailed my hand through the water.
Then the *plunk, plunk* of each oar
hauled over, and placed inside the boat.

Dad cut off a thumb-size slice of tobacco.
"You can row back," he said, "if the tide is right.
If not, I'll take her, or we can wait til the tide turns."
I thought, how odd for him, his daughter gone away
and come back with a southern accent.
I remembered that line from *Gone With the Wind*,

where the black servant says, "I don't know nothin'
bout birthin' no babies, Miss Charlotte."
I'd change that around to, "I don't know nothin'
bout rowin' no dory, Daddy."
But he wouldn't get the joke, besides, we never joked.
Joke was an American word, like cookie, and divorce.

I sat transcribing ballads from cassette tape to page.
He leaned into the doorjamb of my bedroom,
listening to the songs about people he knew
who had died in gales, or sly youths
who had gotten away with something.
I'd say, "What's that, Dad? What's he saying?"
He'd look over his glasses at the machine,
"Clamped ahold to," he'd say, or "Two-buckle spring in your knee,"
a grin spreading into silent memory.
I'd imagine him leaning on a wall at a dance,
waiting to make sure he'd pick the right girl to ask.
Mom said, "Your father would wait til the end of the night
to ask for a dance, right when you'd thought
he never cared for you. A hard man to figure out."

But he was never hard. No. His curse word was "Judas."
His temperament even, his pace full and steady.
At his wake, a man took my hand and said,
"Your father wasn't a man you prayed for, but prayed to."
I turned away. I didn't want him made into a saint,
a man unreachable. I wanted his prejudices, his blind
church-going to meet my sinful life of drinking and manizing.
I wouldn't let him get away from me that easy.
He wouldn't rise at the right hand of anyone.

So I lay in his bed the night he was buried,
remembering his hand in mine, us going for ice cream.

Mom banged on the door, "Come out, you'll drive your nerves bad.
Come out and join the party for your father."
But I lay there surrounded by his few clothes hanging,
the smell of Beaver plug, the crucifix,
the blurred and moving Blessed Virgin dissolving into the Bleeding Heart.
I lay there with his words and stories, ships hove into rocks,
St. Pierre wine in wooden casks, the whaling factory in Rose au Rue,
words I clung to, knowing his passing took away a world.

In the morning, before dawn, a light touch on my head,
a blur of white mist in the room, the faraway words trailing off:
"Get up, now, and let me rest. Go on and help your mother, now."
I threw back the blanket and stumbled into the grey light of day.

Storm

Heavy rain blowing in sheets woke me.
At the window I looked to sea, out past
the harbour wondering if there were boats out,
remembering my father's death and life.

I had walked into the hospital ward
as he was coming up from under the anaesthetic.
His arms stretched over his head tracing
swift, definite movements in the air.

A voice behind me said: "Don't worry, love.
He's mending sails, and then he's tacking home."
I sat down by his bed, tranced as he was,
my eyes following the fragile web of his fingers.

Later when he was himself, he whispered:
"Do you know who that is in the bed across the way?
That's Captain Jim Harris. Go speak the Portuguese to him."

We talked of Aveiro, Oporto, Lisboa,
of the sun, and the wine, and the *fado*.
I felt my father's pride at me speaking Portuguese
to the best sailing captain out of Placentia Bay.

My father so tiny in the bed. Time stealing him from me.
I sat and listened to him and the captain
talk of weather, fish and old schooners—
what he had talked of all his life.

He'd call tonight a bad one.
Hurricane Louis would drive him from his bed,
send him down the hall in his stocking vamps
checking the stove, the doors and windows,
making us warm and watertight.

And tonight
I feel like howling into the fury
to bring him back safe to me.

Longevity and Guts

The Grandparents

Patricia and Thomas

The trader anchored in the harbour and the packmen came out on deck. They spread their wares: Gerald S. Doyle products, jewellery, boots, and clothes. Men rowed out standing up. Since it was a short row, to sit down would look too leisurely. Women never went but only hoped the men got right what they wanted.

Tom wasn't sent but he went. He picked out a ring, a thin gold band, paid in coin and rowed back to the creek half-grinning.

Patsy was turning fish in the hot August sun. Her stomach was swelled only slightly, maybe she could get away with it. Anyway, there was Tom rowing towards her looking cocksure and full of purpose. Winter wouldn't be so hard after all.

The Aunts

Margaret

When Aunt Peg came back home she wanted to be called Margaret. I said ah, but I love the sound of Aunt Peg. She pulled back, set her shoulders just so and exhaled sharp and quick through her nostrils. I never said Peg again.

She threw a glass of beer onto my fifth cousin Anthony's chest, telling him she would not let the Americans be talked about like that. I hear she squared her shoulders, pushed back from the table, went over to my mother's house and changed her airline ticket to get the hell out of Newfoundland and home to Brooklyn.

It irritates my mother to no end that Margaret is so goddammed proud. She won't return. Aunt Lil says she never will. They talk about her in the parlour, I listen from the kitchen. There's more to it than Anthony and the Yanks. That priest on Jude Island who tried to haul her into his bed. She went home, didn't say a word to anyone. He got up at the pulpit the next morning, scared to let another minute pass, and denounced her as a liar who should be tarred and feathered. She hadn't told a soul, though by then it was too late. No one believed her. Her own mother turned away.

Aunt Margaret came back when Grandmother was in the ground. Proud and fierce, she walked through our town butting invisible enemies. I became her silent bodyguard. I wanted her honoured here... but too late, too late, it was far too late.

Now she'll never come back.

She'll be buried in Brooklyn, New York.

Sisley

The family says, "Well sure everyone knows Sis is an alcoholic. She can't get herself to bed without staggering, would get lost if she had to follow a straight line."

Sisley came home once but I never saw her. "Mom, how come I never met Aunt Sis?"

"Your Aunt Sis? I'll tell you why. Because she landed into town, went to Jimmy's, drank gin day and night and then flew off back to New York again. Why she spent almost a thousand dollars to come home and drink the same brand of gin she could get there is beyond me."

I wondered if Aunt Sis ever went to the corner store for mix, ever looked at the Southside Hills from Jim's kitchen window. Jimmy says she still had her black and orange hair, down to her waist, but that

she always wrapped it up before coming out of the bedroom where she
slept with her ninety-year-old mother.

Wish I could have seen her, cigarette between her lips, the
curling smoke making her eye pinch up as she folded out the
cards in solitaire, and sloshed the plastic stirrer into gin and ice.

Lillian

Everyone wanted to get away. There was a whole slew of us lined up,
signing our name on visa applications. Above all else, get out. Why turn
over one more maggoty fish, iron one more shirt, scrub one more floor
for two dollars a month? Give me a warm Jewish restaurant on Eighth
Avenue where you get respect and tips.

Aunt Lil worked hard, married Pete Wasinski. I remember him
in the grass, under the dogberry tree, coins falling from his pockets like
bread crumbs, laughing as the wind stood his hair straight. Mom said
that when he died the shoes blew off his feet from his massive heart
attack. Well, he did have such a big heart, making sure we kids found
the silver in the grass.

Aunt Lil married again, a man from home. Came back to
Newfoundland saying she could never stay in the States anymore: "All
the small town feel is gone from Manhattan."

Lillian, oldest daughter, never had children or a pet, but has a
full-length sealskin coat.

"The only thing your grandmother gave us," she told me, "was
longevity and guts. That was all she gave us."

Ellen

In the snapshot she has her sweater pinned at the neck, but her arms
aren't in the sleeves. This strikes me as unlike her so I look for more. It

is some sort of courtyard where she stands, drooping veronicas lined against a black fence. Her smile is a question of delight, like when someone says, "You are beautiful," and you say, "Pardon?" because you want to hear it again.

The wind is blowing in the photo, her skirt tail is kicking up behind her. At her feet a small dog barks silently and she leans into a man who looks like Trotsky (he stayed at the Cochrane Hotel on his way to Mexico, and she worked next door).

I asked her about this once and she gave me that smile again and brushed her fingers across her lips as if the room was bugged. "Facts," she said. "Oh my, why do you always need the facts, you with all these photographs?"

The Interview

Of course I remember, she said,
I had just got aboard the boat and I was lost.
I had covered the first deck and then I thought
I'd try the upper one. I was on my way up the stairs
and he was on his way down to the lower.
He had on a raglan, a black raglan and he wore
black-framed eyeglasses. I remember thinking that
his glasses matched his coat. He never nodded or spoke
and I never either. And when I saw him again to O'Keefe's
years later I thought to myself, this is not the first time
I'm after seeing you. But I couldn't place him then.
It was only on my wedding night that I put it together.
That he was your father.

I have the microphone set up on the small, square table
in the parlour.

What use is this kind of information to what you're doing?
What are you doing anyway?
Why do you want to know this stuff?

I just want to know, I tell her.
It might not be any use, I just want to know.

I had you cut out for teaching, she said,
the way you loved notes and facts and how
you used to babysit the Yanks' youngsters and
be reading to them and getting paid in Nancy Drew books.
I thought you'd end up with a good job in some school.
It seems to me you have to be always chasing after work

with what you do, whatever it is. I mean, it's up to yourself,
I'm only saying.

I tell her I prefer this even though I can't
call it anything either.
I couldn't be in a building all day, I say.

Sure you are anyway, aren't you? she says
and holds my eye. She's got a point.

I can come and go, I say.

Coming and going, she says, only leads to drafts.
And drafts lead to colds, and colds to pneumonia.

Thomas

He wanted to be a body man in the car racket,
get his own cars and strip them down
then rebuild them like new.

I only encouraged him, started learning the year
of the cars and riddling them off.
As we'd turn the curve around Point Verde pond
and meet a 57 Chevy I'd call it out,
he'd purse a kiss at me and I'd edge in closer.
That was before seat belts.

Sometimes we'd stop the car below the downs
and devour each other whole.
That's the way it was.

I met him the other day in the parking lot
of the hardware store. His children were holding onto his legs,
their red heads aflame like his, still on fire in the evening sun.
He leaned onto the hood of his 62 Ford pickup and said,
you're still the same, girl, still the same.

Why don't you ask me what I'm driving, I said.
Well, all right then, what is it?
A horse and saddlebags, and in summer
a 650 Triumph opened up on Ship Cove Hill.

He threw his flaming head back and laughed.
It was an old joke about dreams.
I might have asked was he still a body man,
but I didn't. I wanted to imagine he still was.

Pitchfork

It is said that a pitchfork landed us here.
The old man got in a row with his step-mother
and . . . sowzo! Over the hedge he flung her.

That was somewhere in Tipperary,
where he came from to here. He hid in the woods
(it was all woods) down in what's now mash.

I heard tell of it by hiding under the table
same way he hid in the woods.
I hid only to hear, not because I kilt anyone.
I hid to hear what the old people were talking about,

even though children were to be
seen and not heard, and not
listening to how they got here,
either by birth or any other way.

So old Bartley came from inland Ireland
to the wind-swept savage coast of the Cape Shore,
cleared twelve acres of the best land and
had twelve children, cleared his name by
clearing land and digging in.

And here I sit, at the table tonight, not under it,
telling you, as the sun sinks golden on the mash
two hundred years later, and we whisper his name
in the hushed room, in the golden room,
we whisper as if they were finally coming after him.

Love

1
You might wonder why the place
has so many bachelors,
but the thing is he wasn't allowed out after
ten o'clock until he was forty-seven years old,
and only then because his mother had passed away.

The old people were strict, they had old ways.
He had to be in for the rosary. She declared it
a mortal sin to kneel down without him.

She never approved of anyone, no girl
was good enough, so he got stranded
with a kitchen full of buddies
and a bottle of rum.

And there was a certain upholding to do
after his parents passed on. It was the house
where confessions were heard before
they got the boxes in the church,

and the baptisms held, and a room
had to be kept for the priest.
Hard to court women, after a spell,
and then all the priests drank with him too.

So he grew tall, and lonely on long winter evenings.
He liked the female company, the way
a woman could be at the kitchen table
that a man couldn't, the air made softer.

When he was eighty-two he said to me one time
I have never seen a woman's chest, no I never have.
We were friends for ten years then, I loved him.
I unbuttoned my blouse and smiled at him.

And do you know when he saw me
with my forty-three-year-old breasts
there at the kitchen table
he cried a tear and he told me I was beautiful.

2

At first your daybed was a piece of board
nailed into the side of the wall,
then your sister from the states saw one
in an antique shop in Delaware and
had it sent. You wouldn't lie on it,
only sit. Be afraid they'd think
I was Cleopatra, Queen of the Nile,
you said. It went to the shed
leaned up against your dory.

In came the chesterfield with the bright
blue flowers and yellow background.
Now it has a dent in the middle
from your sharp hips and the one arm
worn down from your head resting
into the bowl of your hands.

In winter it is your nightbed too,
with the old navy stock blanket

thrown over. You smell like my father—
warm, old, musky. Wood smoke grained
in your skin, stove oil soaked through your pores.

Your kitchen is your world, its once
white high-glossed walls now tinted amber
like the brun cafes in Amsterdam.
Chrome table, wood chairs, Holy Mary,
daybed, stove, cupboard, woodbox, telephone.

I doze sitting up, startle, you smile,
say, Now you know why I need a bed there, girl.
I float in your kitchen, we talk little,
sweat a lot, gulp hot tea, and watch
the sun set into the sea.

3
You sat at the table where you always sit
that morning I entered your kitchen
for the last time with you in it.

It was a Monday and the first time I'd come into
your kitchen on a Monday morning without the smell
of Javex and the sound of the old ringer washer clunking away.
Perhaps the first Monday in 90-odd years that it wasn't wash-Monday.

You sat and looked at me coming through the doorjamb
and I looked at your suitcase tied round with a bit of rope,
two cardboard boxes tied round with a bit of rope, and your cap
and winter coat laid on top. It stopped me short there in the doorway.

I knew you were going. I knew this was the day.
But the awful stillness. You shook your head at me
and I knew you were baffled by your own sadness, for you were
always up for everything, a change, anything.

We didn't speak but sat there waiting for Wishey to come—
him to take you to live in town, me to live on up the road without you.

What do I do now if I can't get around that knot,
or, worse, get to make a proper one?
Who can I ask where the wind is off of,
where the path to the inner pond begins,

and what was old Bartley's step-mother's name
that he pitchforked over the hedge in Tipperary?
What to do when the only way forward for me
is back, back in time through you and this house.

4
Now your room is like a whistle, clean as a shriek,
and a television on your dresser and the brown suitcase
(rope still around it) up on top of the wardrobe,
an indoor toilet, you show me, happy like a boy with his first apartment.
You flick on the stove elements and wait
until they glow red, and dishes supplied by management
(no more Chinese blue to tell the future by), and no need
hauling wood: you pat the thermostat.

Can't say much for the tap water though, you tell me,
so Bridget brings me in a drop from Point Verde.
And you sit down next to me on the bed and swing
your long legs and put your arm around my shoulder,
and when I lean in to rest my head that's
when I know, but I don't say a word.

You've lost your smell. The wood-smoke, the oil, the musk,
the years, the years and years. So, I ask, the shower then,
that must be a treat?
Ah yes, you laugh, the shower. That's the first time I had a wash
since I fell overboard in 1942. I'll have to beat the women off now.

Wind in the Old Town

1
It was the storm that never arrived.
You couldn't call strong winds a storm—
well maybe if there was rain, or sleet, or snow,

but this was early fall, these were delayed August
breezes that got lost somewhere off land
in summer, and like late patrons at the theatre
now scurried for their seats,

and the air hung up in alley-ways,
in sails not yet hauled in, and under
the backs of unbuttoned coats.

It made hair stand up from under
the pole of the head, made it flare out the back
and up, up, a baton invisible, conducting the invisible.

It had the run of Water Street.
We buckled under it like miming
kicks in the solar plexus.

We couldn't talk, the wind stole our words,
whipped them from our mouths and threw them
at the wrong ears so people became delirious
with information that had nothing to do with them.

Some, the drunk and the very young,
levelled arms out at their sides
and played at being airplanes.

Canopies flapped wildly, then lay flattened,
skirts lifted around thighs and trousers billowed
like stilt men in the circus.

Such was the course of the wind
that night in early fall
when St. John's was an international port,
and pulsed with a dozen tongues.

Now, all has died down to a terrible calm.
A breeze is this city now,
sifting the industry of bringing people in
and getting them to stay the night,

but at one time
you could hear drums.

2
The drum was Spanish
from the north, Galicia.
A wooden box hung by rope about his neck
and two drum sticks rapped sharply.

He was followed by a bagpiper
unlike any I had ever heard,
a thin whine, more Arabic than highland or Ireland,
charming cobras and pale-skinned women
up, up in any direction,
pied piper.

I danced because I cannot sing
and was admitted to the band.

That night on Water Street, the wind
laughed and laughed along with us.
People stared. Some joined in—
Carnival in St. John's town, a party
linking the land and the sea.

Oranges in Barranco do Velho

Oranges hung in trees.
A simple enough sentence,
still life even.
Very still the oranges hung just
over our heads
with two green leaves
slanting downwards.

I plucked them by reaching up.
No one shooed us off,
no one took a shot at us,
so we sat on the wet grass
and let the juice leak over our knees
and down the insides of our arms,
two very pale white people
suckling on the warm fruit,
twelve hours after seeing snow fall.

Afterwards the leaves would line my pockets
and be slipped into pillowcases.

Al-Gharb

The night is indigo and filled
with the scent of warm flowers,
a blanket of scent in the night air
that moves under my tongue,
into your hair.

We climb the soft square cobblestone
into the heart of Silves, old Moorish capital
of Al-Gharb, and the night wraps us,
circles us, hauls us in.

Underfoot, the small square stones of the sidewalk
soft as soapstone.
I take off my sandals in the dark.
I walk the winding streets and the uneven stone
rocks my body, softens my body.

I hear oranges drop to the earth
in the far-off orchards,
the soft thump and roll
of oranges in the dark night.

For Anita

In the soft rain there on the balcony in Oporto
all of us were happy, happy with expectation—
this beautiful country, so open for us, so full of us already.
Take me back to that beautiful country, oh my heart.

You and me Anita, at the table with the senhora so severe,
with the chicken and the perfumed white wine, the bread,
the ghost-white cheese. That was enough, that was us in an afternoon,
a lifetime of history behind us, on the heels of ourselves,

knowing we trailed after ghosts, that they lay in vaults
like bottles of old port hauled up to the light.
We sat, expecting nothing and anything, and the ghosts spoke
because we cannot live unless they whisper, unless they shout,

and echo on the stone squares, and bang into our hearts.

Seaweed on Point Lance Beach

Great heavy mounds, soggy,
hove up, pulsing an inner life
of grit, sand, sea-lice, and starfish.

The smell is all brine,
the feel rubber,
sea-plant torn away from sunkers,
from wrecks of schooners,
from floating, floating, floating,
waving long arms, waving.

Dark, deep red, deep rust red,
a wall of food, of fertilizer
building up, growing with every wave,
washed up, drug in, pounded down,
but rising up, swelling into breathing hills.

Later, in the bath, the sea swirls around me,
ocean secrets enter me. I go under,
where iodine is narcotic, where
irish moss is skin graft.

I surface with kelp still clinging
as the bath water goes out the bay.

Contacts

I never knew such a thing existed
I swear to God I never.

I was into Irving's and she came up to our table
and her blue eyes flooded me, I drowned in the blue.
I said, Oh my God, I never saw such blue eyes
before in my life, my God Almighty, I said,
you have the bluest eyes I ever saw. I was astounded.

She looked to the left and then to the right
to see who was listening, but I couldn't stop,
I had my head up almost in under her chin.
I mean, I said, I thought Elizabeth Taylor had blue eyes!
I thought Bob Dylan had blue eyes but...

She slapped the menu down on the table at us,
the heavy plastic thudding like a nun's strapper.
They're contact lenses, she hissed, they're goddamn
contact lenses. Do you want water with your meal?

When she gave us the bill she had her glasses on
and her eyes were grey or green or something.
I could hardly look at her. I thought she was lovelier but
I didn't dare tell her that then.

Fireweed

for Bridget Pegeen Kelly

No, Bridget Pegeen, fireweed isn't the colour of fire
and it isn't purple either.
It's purplish-pink, and yes, it's delicate looking.
The petals look like they'd avalanche, like
to touch one would cause a riot.
The stalk is tough as seasoned leather;
I could make a clothesline out of a string of them.
They grow, like blueberries, where there's been a fire.
Fireberries. They stand tall in fields and proclaim themselves wild.
Of savage origin. Beauty's breathless rampage.

Patrick's Cove

There is a visitation of light
upon the bare wall, a perfect rectangle
of a picture of light. As you cross
to the ashtray your head turns gold
and your eyes sear red. You could be one
of the devils in the corner
of Hieronymus Bosch's Hell.

This is the September light that falls
piercing with its cooler edge, falls
through the loose clapboard of root cellars
and strikes upon a corner abandoned for a hundred years
but never by the light.

It slants the kitchen table just so, tilting it,
trying to convince you you are on water.

And into the valley of this lonely cove
it slices the curved hills and seems for a second
to remember a glorious past.
When all else ends, people trickling out,
that light will still make its mark, over and over,
and never once the same.

The Tilts, Point Lance

Nights like this you could forget
you had a wife, kids, a town,
the sky so big, the ocean always there,
man alone to think about mortality.

Inside, the smell of tobacco, dirty hair,
rubbed-in cod guts, and diesel grease,
margarine, and burnt wool, stale rum sometimes,
grunts and nods enough, curses to punctuate.

Women want more: curtains, salt shakers,
nightclothes, verbs, wildflowers, french safes.
Here it's stove, bunks, table, chairs.

A grin though going back on Saturday,
always enough fish, it's Cape St. Mary's.
A grin in my lapel and, make no mistake,
glad to be back to civilization

one mile up the road.

"begin with the world: let it be small enough"
Jorie Graham

There isn't a teaspoon of snow
anywhere. Instead tires are hissing
on Duckworth Street. We're amazed and
everybody my age says, don't say we won't pay
for this. We say we're not going paying
for this, no sir, even if we are snowed
under in a week's time. We'll shovel with a smile
on our lips and pat our purses. We're oblivious and
heading to Spain somewhere in our minds all the time anyway.

Call it a resolution: we don't live in weather.
And don't we think the Christmas lights are bougainvillea.
Oh that word! It fills the mouth like an armful of themselves.

Summer under Winter

O unworn world enrapture me
Patrick Kavanagh

January and your cheeks are red
and there's a blue hairy cap on your head
but the sun is a great white ball on the hill
and we're not cold at all, even standing still.

We let ourselves fall to the frozen ground in laughing fits
and we make hot love through our mitts.
There is an airplane flying low with a summer sound
and a warm smoothness in the air from the ground.

Oh the ice is delicious to crunch with our warm teeth
as we stamp and dance to thaw out our feet.
Amid all this white we hear the cracking of the river
that perhaps we started because we broke off a sliver.

O world, so white and cold and warm.

Tango

for Robert Duvall

everything is perfect:
the woman, the man,
the music, the dance

for once the breath
is held in that catch
that is breathing in no breath
and the mind is the soul

the child of yourself is
back in your lap,
the outside is in
and fits   perfectly

you know that life,
once gone, has returned,
sits down next
to you   sings

Gull, Crow, at Table

Shaking out the mat I don't
know if that's what set them off.

One so raucous that a rent
in stillness is all it shows,
the other helpless, calling out, wondering
is the world still there.

Behind my door is all they don't know.
I imagine the crow at table,
disappointed in the fare, the gull:
"go on now, sure it's lovely."

The pure black and the white and grey,
the eyes so terrifyingly there,
the thrill of the outside in, the
wondering now how to live.

Placentia

(after Elizabeth Bishop's "Casabianca")

Love's the girl stood on the rocky beach
watching the tidal wave gather strength.
She is trying to recite "The girl stood on
the rocky beach." Love's the daughter
    stood stuttering under the nun's glare
    while the wave broke heavy on the shore.

Love's the stubborn girl, the beach,
even the running townspeople, who
would like to have gone to school, too,
    or had a reason to stay
    home. And love's the swimming girl.

Looking on the Water

Bird Island Resort, St. Bride's

This arch of white fence
against the sky keeps
the ocean out,
keeps the sky away.

The winter sky, so pale, so
white it blends in with the
fence, is leaning on the fence
like an old man in summertime.

The gulls don't mind the
fence. They're all over the
place, same with the wind,
but just now a gull slipped

on some air current (like
black ice you don't see),
careened away into the drop-off
of cliff below the lookout
with steps descending to seaweed, to

a winter beach so far down, so
lonely, so cold even the gulls can't pitch there.

St. Bride's

One room, one position which is frontward.
What lies ahead is ocean, sky, snow and a flashing
red light. It is winter, it is north, bleak, cold,
grey, white, bright. All that.

What more it is is space. The Cape road ahead blocked.
In fact there is no road, summer is erased,
the birds gone, flowers asleep, like
when someone leaves you and takes love with them or
dumps it at your feet in a great cold sack.

It is awhile before the eyes adjust to nothing,
to seeing how much is there. It takes a trying on of
patience, a wrestle with your indignant soul,
nerve.

Try standing (if the wind backs off) a little
at a time, only don't move, let
the time add up, let it
have its say. I swear
this is the way to love,
to regain the winter, the north,
the frozen earth on which you stand.

For Val Ryan

Always I'll remember you
adjusting your glasses with your thumb
and index finger, thick coke-bottle glass
in black frames.

When you were drunk you'd tell a story
that went all over the place, and you'd say
I'm rambling, but you see this is the story of
a rambling Irish lad, see.

Nobody could ramble like you, Val
last of the St. Mary's Bay Irish-Newfoundland gentlemen.

Your sister said the government had you dead
a year before your time.
You got your death certificate in the mail, read it,
took down your fiddle and played yourself a lament.

In the hospital your thick wavy hair fell back
and your body heaved with the pressure of holding on.
I saw death stalk, wanting you,
but not more than us, Val.

Me and Ye

I called your dog a she
before I knew she was one,

but sure she had to be a she,
didn't she?

One day will you take she
to the seashore?

Sure, you will, I'm sure,

and, ah, would you mind
if I went along with ye

to see the sea and ye
walking alongside she?

His Match

What he told me in a pub on Bere Island, West Cork, October 2002

He first saw her at Castletownbere fair.
He was over selling a calf, they took a liking
to one another and after he came home he
asked his father would she suit. He said he knew
her history and it was good. So, come Shrovetide
their hands were clasped, the match was made,
and the next day they had a fine wedding. Two sheep
killed, four barrels of porter drunk.
The match was good. It took.

The Wind Joined Us on Bere Island

We stuck into the wind as if we were
telling it there was no sense
blowing against us. There was a mission,
something had to be done, and we
were the girls to do it. The pilot
was a young fellow, maybe eighteen,
a pup, but a water dog.

We were coming down from Cork city
to Bere Island and the whole way
the wind kept yelling "go back, get."
On board the boat we stayed outside—
three dolmens on a watery plain.

We slung our bags onto the open deck
and stayed with them. The run was short,
the rain was soft, but the wind,
oh the wind was serious.

On the other side it was all a scramble,
unload the bags, jump to the wharf,
get the car, and by then the wind
didn't mind us. It got on our side,
moved us along.

Entering Galway

the usual is news enough
Mary Oliver

Relief of water after all week inland.
Sharp reeds, sweet green off Nun's Island,
swirl of town in pre-tourist ease.

The woman next to me on the bus blesses
herself at every church, graveyard and shrine
to Our Lady. She says she is always on the go
to pilgrimages, Lourdes and Fatima.

I've a devotion to Mary, she tells me.
Once, she said, this was Holy Ireland.
And now? Different now.
When she gets off in Limerick she hopes
Our Lady will gave me safe passage through Ireland.
Mind the young fellows in Galway, she says.
They have no religion.

The Stealing of Crom Dubh's Head

The ruins of the medieval church stood
in the shadows of the pagan world. They loomed,
but not tall enough, not power enough to stop
old Dubh's head coming loose like a rotten molar.

It was wriggled and pried and...yanked.
And he a tooth god!

The pilgrims walked round and round
the dark crooked one with their caskets
on the way to the hole in the ground
at the start of the pilgrimage to Mount Brandon
on Crom Dubh Sunday, for the festival of Lughnasa,
where St. Brendan and the pagan met,

the latter hauled off by thieves in the night
in the 1970s
when there's no fear of nothing.

The Cows Were There

Bere Island, West Cork, Ireland, November 2003

In the kitchen with just a low light on
I watched the sky break open into the day
and I heard the cows rustle through the brittle leaves
before I saw them. They came out of the old orchard
into the day and stood and stared at me,
seven of them. I said What? and they blinked.

Once a great grey heron dropped out of the sky
into Bere Haven inlet just as the sun was opening
orange right behind it. The heron looked like he was
called in to report to the sun.
When those cows realized I had nothing to offer,
they looked disappointed and moved
away from the window to the other side of the house.

Simone stands at the half-door with the top
half opened and latched back. Her arms are folded over
her chest and it is half dark behind her. "Don't you
love the cows, Mommy, how they're just there?" I'm
in the kitchen with the heron in case it flies off,

for it is there still, only shifting from leg to leg now,
and the cows there, there all day for one whole week.
We are in their pasture.

The lane we walk up has hidden ditches covered in gorse
and hawthorn, deep ditches well hidden which is why we have to walk.
I ran the car into the ditch grinding the rim, so here we are in the

half-dark walking so she can wait with Silvana's children
for the bus to the ferry.

The walk back is full of cows and the sun really coming up
over the inlet and spraying out over the barren hills of West Cork.
Across the harbour I see the house Neil Jordan bought for his mother
after he did good with *The Crying Game*. Old ascendency homes dot
the shore and there's the heron again, ascending himself, toes delicately
reaching for the rounded rocks on the shore.

My hands are in my pockets but I'm not cold.
It is more the need to place my whole self
squarely, straight up and down into what is new,
never mind the need to connect again with what is old,
with what could have been me.

Your Country

Who started this anyway?
I want to know.

You're the one's married
and bored and lonely and
romantic as hell
and meeting me at the train saying
I've arranged time off.

Not that I'm innocent, far
from it. I'm fifty-two.
But still, you had no right
to turn my head while
twisting your ring
so it caught the light sometimes and
sometimes gathered tarnish,

same as how you hold
passports for two places
and don't love either.

Long Distance Lover

I wish I had a long distance lover,
someone I could write letters to.
Darling, when I meet you
move out of town.

Is it that we stumble into love?

Is it that we stumble into love?
Somewhere, in ancient times,
there must have been proverbs stacked
up in memory that kept the old ones
wiser even when they were young.

Should we make a study of it, my love,
say this time we will not skip stones
over reason, say we will take the time,
this time, steady our hands, learn how to breathe.

I'll consider anything except that you
didn't happen. Even self-denial is better than
the blank stare of a half-heart.

If the old ones came back,
would we thank or curse them?

Evening and it is always like this

Evening and it is always like this:
half-answered prayers offered up again
in a new light, disappointment magnified
through repetition. There is a photo of you

outdoors looking skyward, jaw softened
with shadow, silhouette of fir trees across
your chest, you in a window, you always
behind something, eyes cast up, that search.

I want to tell you it is not beyond,
that thin plate of glass is bullshit armor.
I want to smash it because this love
turned into a mission when I wasn't looking.

I want destruction to make something good happen
once and for all, to say look down, outward,

find me.

Andalusian Rain

Sitting in the old Dick's at the window
the day before you leave for Spain
wind rattles at the glass, rat-a-tat-tat.
You draw out the time for the Seguiriya,
the Buleria, and the Soleares.
I watch your long fingers beat out
the rhythm for me, rat-a-tat-tat,
and my heart knocks against my bones.

I tell you about Cabot in Seville
talking to Ferdinand and Isabella,
of Cabot in Lisbon trying to get a ship,
someone to believe in him. I tell you of Lisbon,
the fado, the Alfama, the Portuguese on the waterfront.
You tell me of Seville, about the handsome man
with the scar from eye to jawbone, your search for teachers.

I trace on the map Lisbon to Seville,
trace your back without touching you.

Three of us sit in the bar on Water Street,
you, your husband, me. In the bar where you
want to dance the flamenco when you return.
I make the arrangements. It is easy. Because I love you.
Will he kill me for loving you? No, I will make him understand.

I talk about Cabot, about Vasco da Gama, Corte Real,
and the Cape Shore. How schooners from here traded
with Spain and Portugal. I remember an orange
with a leaf on the stem, port wine the colour

of blood and earth mixed. I say funny
you going back to Seville, me going back to Lisbon,
funny, this year when everyone comes here
and instead we are going back, funny, but I cry.

You will never love me. But you will.
I feel your tears. I see your head thrown back
into the soft Andalusian rain. I love you because
you feel everything and want more.

Before we left the café you asked me how
my father died, if he was with me.
My story was sad, tragic, and you left the table
tears streaming down your face. Then my heart
could not hold the beating, then it died
a long death waiting for you to come back,
to the table, to this island, come back
so that I can feel life again.

Alone I sit and stack the notes,
the voyages, 1496, 1497, 1498. The attempt,
the success, the disappearance. I make my reservation
for Lisbon. I sail across the ocean, *The Mattew*
a ghost ship passing me in the night.
You there in the soft Andalusian spring
trailing your hair through a mimosa breeze.
I trace on the map Lisbon to Seville
trace your back without touching you, through tears.

Acknowledgments

Several of these poems have appeared in the following: *TickleAce*; *Pottersfield Portfolio*; *Words Out There*, edited by Jeanette Lynes; *Signatures: Newfoundland Women Artists and Writers, Newfoundland Quarterly*.

"Storm" and "Ellen" (as "In the Snapshot") were published in *In The Old Country of My Heart*, St. John's: Killick, 1996.

One source of "His Match" is oral; another is written, and lost. When and if the lost is found, it will be gratefully acknowledged.

Very special thanks to Stan Dragland, Helen Humphreys, Lisa Moore, Venessa Bennett, Monique Tobin, Michael McGrath, Agnes Walsh Sr., Pre-confederation Newfoundlanders of Placentia Bay, Newfoundland and Labrador Arts Council, Canada Council for the Arts.

$\mathcal{A}$gnes Walsh was born and raised in Placentia, Newfoundland. An actor, playwright, storyteller, and poet, she has worked in theatre for over thirty years. She has won several awards for her poetry, which has appeared in various literary magazines, and has read widely in North America and Europe. Her work has been translated into French, Portuguese, and Icelandic. Walsh's first collection of poems, In the Old Country of My Heart (Killick Press, 1996), sold out and was reprinted in 1998. She was named the inaugural St. John's Poet Laureate in 2006.

GOING AROUND WITH BACHELORS BY AGNES WALSH
CD TRACK LIST

Track				
Track	1	Title Credit		7 sec
	2	I Solemn	3 min	3 sec
	3	The Laying Out, 1956		32 sec
	4	Almost a Word	3 min	17 sec
	5	Dad and the Fridge Box *		58 sec
	6	Dad and the Fridge Box	3 min	8 sec
	7	One night as the moon shone **	3 min	12 sec
	8	Introducing ballads from Patsy Judge*	1 min	45 sec
	9	Going Around with Bachelors	1 min	18 sec
	10	To Boston		55 sec
	11	Homecoming to the End	4 min	34 sec
	12	Storm	1 min	47 sec
	13	Longevity and Guts	6 min	44 sec
	14	The Interview	1 min	55 sec
	15	Blooming Bright Star from Belle Isle **	4 min	45 sec
	16	Thomas	1 min	30 sec
	17	Pitchfork	1 min	20 sec
	18	Pitchfork *		17 sec
	19	Love	6 min	1 sec
	20	For Anita	1 min	1 sec
	21	Patrick's Cove	1 min	10 sec
	22	The Tilts, Point Lance	1 min	6 sec
	23	"begin with the world: let it be small enough"		48 sec
	24	Summer under Winter	1 min	0 sec
	25	Gull, Crow, at Table		48 sec
	26	Bonny Bunch of Roses **	3 min	7 sec
	27	Placentia		42 sec
	28	Looking on Water		56 sec
	29	St. Bride's	1 min	25 sec
	30	For Val Ryan	1 min	0 sec
	31	The Cows Were There	2 min	34 sec
	32	The Prison of Newfoundland **	4 min	36 sec
	33	Me and Ye	2 min	3 sec
	34	The Interview *		35 sec

* Asides: Agnes Walsh speaking with Janet Russell and Simone Savard-Walsh.
** Ballads, arranged by Pamela Morgan and sung by Simone Savard-Walsh.